# Opening the Present

How to Teach Your People the Time Management Secrets of the Top 1% Most Productive People in the World

The Guru Leadership Series

# Welcome to The Guru Leadership Series

For great free content and additional information, email us at **ask@whatthegurusays.com**.

Or

Join us on Facebook at What The Guru Says

At the end of the book, we have added some great tools to help you and your business, and to assist in teaching these concepts.

J. H. Dies retains the exclusive rights to any use and application or adaptation of this book

Opening the Present: How to Teach Your People the Time Management Secrets of the Top 1% Most Productive People in the World. Copyright© 2016 by J. H. Dies All rights reserved. Printed in the United States of America. No part of this book may be used or reproduced in any manner whatsoever without written permission except in the case of brief quotations embodied in critical articles and reviews.

FIRST EDITION
ISBN-13: 978-1540690715

Library of Congress Cataloging in Publication data has been applied for

The Guru Mission

Our Mission is to improve businesses and their people with simple, actionable ideas.

This book contains some great extras. If you would like electronic copies of these materials in editable form, send us an email with Guru TM in the subject line to ask@whatthegurusays.com

# This Guru Book

This book is intended to be read in an hour or so, and then revisited as a reference tool as needed. There are a number of useful tools in the back of the book which may be employed as you see fit. You will note that there are many different examples from different industries. These are designed to provide clarity but the solutions offered have broad application to many different business types.

One of the reasons time management is such a challenge for leaders is that causes of poor time management can be widely varied, but the symptoms are the same.

Your employee's production is off relative to the talent you have scouted in making the decision to hire him. Is he a poor project manager? Does she prioritize incorrectly? Is he a perfectionist who is getting poor return on his time investment? Perhaps she underestimates the time it takes to complete tasks? Does he understand delegating?

The reality is that you or your employee could have any or all of these problems. This book is designed to simplify how you think about time, but it is not intended to be a statistical analysis of employee time consumption.

Read it with a mind toward issue spotting, and use guru techniques to get more out of your employees, which will improve your profitability, and your employee's income potential. Enjoy!

# Table of Contents

1. The Why – Creating Clarity ………………………………..1

2. The How Part 1 – Isolating What Matters ………………......7

3. The How Part 2 – Watching Time Like It's Money………...13

4. Slaying Most of the Technology Dragon …………………..18

5. Embracing What's Left of the Dragon……………………..23

6. The Gardener Who Changed the World…………………...28

7. Why Top Performers Don't Delegate and How to Fix it ….34

8. The Waiter's Secret to Telephone Time Management……..38

9. Sharpening The Ax ………………………………………..41

10. The Quiet Danger of Superfluous Choices………………....46

# Chapter 1    The Why

> "You can't depend on your eyes when your imagination is out of focus."  -Mark Twain

You know how important time is, so we won't waste it on clichés, assuming instead that you know that, or you wouldn't have purchased this book. You may have even realized the irony of massively long, convoluted books on time management. What you may not know is that one of the greatest reasons for poor time management in your organization could be you, the leader.

## THE PROBLEM

Simply put, your employees may not have sufficient understanding of what not to do.

## THE EXAMPLE: SALES

In sales for example, activities should be limited to two ends, generation of revenue or the creating of wildly satisfied customers (in that order). If a particular task does not further either of those ends, it is a waste of time, and your people should know that. This is the why, and it must be crystal clear.

Ask your people what is expected of them. I dare you. You will get, "I am here to do a good job," or "I am here to set 25 appointments per week." Both of these are terrible answers.

The first is terrible because of its ambiguity. The second is poor, because it is simply wrong. If the revenue goal is a million dollars a month for the team, one employee could set 10 appointments, and another 100. Without more information, no one could guess who generated more revenue.

The tendency of poor leaders is to set ill-defined goals based on expediency. It would be common to say, "Our average sale is $50,000 in revenue, and we close two in 10 appointments, therefore we need 100 appointments to hit our revenue goal." An even worse manager would reward someone for merely setting 150 appointments.

In this example, the only thing that matters is revenue. The message to employees therefore, should be, "appointments are immaterial, unless they yield signed engagements." This encourages your people to focus their time on quality appointments. It also causes introspection into why certain appointments close at a higher rate, or why others yield more revenue. This is critical to sales productivity, and you as the leader should not be the only person thinking about it.

It may be that the reason for only closing two in ten appointments is that lead qualification is insufficient (poor use of time), or it may be that there is poor preparation for sales meetings themselves. Everyone involved would clearly prefer fewer meetings with a better closure rate, or higher revenue. This is how time should properly be spent.

# THE SOLUTION

While this example relates to sales, every employee at your organization ought to be able, in one sentence, to state a particular why. Assistants might be there to increase productivity in their sales rep from 1x to 1.5x. The irony of poor time management in your top performers will be addressed in a later chapter, but one of the highest returns your firm will ever get on time management is to improve their efficiency.

Getting your people to focus on the why takes three steps.

1. Each employee must have a simple, measurable purpose. (with takeaways and timelines)

2. That employee must be bought in, that is they must AGREE with the goal, and believe it is attainable.

3. There must be enforcement by YOU.

So how do you do that?

Since revenue goals are very specific, and generally pretty clear, we won't use them as an example here. Let's use an apparently immeasurable goal from this chapter as an example of how to handle this situation, (in particular the goal of creating wildly satisfied clients). For clarity we will use the numbers from the steps above to illustrate.

1. Each employee is responsible for creating wildly satisfied clients at 60% rate, which can be objectively determined based upon client behavior. (For our purposes we will say testimonials, referrals, and repeat engagements). The determination of whether a client is wildly satisfied will occur with 30 days of completed delivery of our product/service. This second part is critical to the equation because it gives clarity and creates urgency in the creation of wildly satisfied clients.

2. "Ms. Employee, is it reasonable given the quality of our product/service, and your client relationships that we should be able to get 6 out of 10 clients to send a short letter recommending our work, provide a referral contact, and/or use us again?" And let's assume the employee says, "Yes." Obviously a "no," here yields a great conversation as to why the employee believes this is not possible and/or learning moment for the leader to work through how it is. [The author highly recommends *Raving Fans*, by Ken Blanchard for greater depth at how to do this]

3. Upon completion of the sales cycle, and after product or services are delivered, measure this conversion rate. If it is consistently higher adjust the goal. If it is consistently lower, and the employee is experienced, the leader should investigate to find the cause of failure. This is the most important step of the three. The idea is to create constant dialogue about what is expected, and whether expectations are being met, so that your people are holding themselves and each other accountable. New employees will see that this is just the way things are, and then you will have traction. When employees demonstrate poor time management, simple questions about whether what they are doing contributes to their why will help them to recalibrate.

This process may seem obvious, but it will change how your team speaks to each other and clients. You will have employees talking to their colleagues, and your customers about how they want them to be wildly satisfied, and something special will happen.

## TAKEAWAYS

- Leadership could be to blame for time inefficiency
- Clear measureable goals with buy in, takeaways, and timelines are critical to creating focus and urgency with time management
- Following up and enforcement will help to create habits and a self-sustaining system.

# Chapter 2 The How Part 1

*There is nothing less productive than to make more efficient what should not be done at all." - Peter Drucker*

It is not enough to tell employees what not to do, or to explain how what they are doing may not be the best use of their time. If that is the only thing you do, you will be doing it all the time. To improve your efficiency, and theirs, you have to teach your people how to do this for themselves.

This book will draw from examples offered by other thought leaders on the subject of time management, because these folks have tested and proven the techniques at issue, and at a very high level.

No discussion of time management would be complete without some discussion of the Eisenhower matrix. It is a well-recognized tool for prioritizing tasks from a time management perspective. Steven Covey does a fantastic job on breaking it down in detail in his book *Seven Habits of Highly Effective People*, but that level of detail is unnecessary for our work here.

If it makes a U.S. President better at time management, it can certainly help your business.

The quick and dirty of the matrix works like this:

|  | Urgent | Not Urgent |
|---|---|---|
| Important | Do | Decide |
| Not Important | Delegate | Delete |

If only teaching it were this easy. A ton of books on time management have discussed this concept, and many top performing organizations actively apply its principles daily.

We have tried a number of different ways to teach this, and found only one that is effective.

## THE PROBLEM

Employees understand the concepts of importance and urgency, and how to handle them, but the application of these principles to their work, specifically in defining what tasks fit in these categories, often reflects a huge disconnect between the team and leadership.

## THE EXAMPLE: PROJECT MANAGEMENT

When project managers get new assignments, regardless of the type of project, there tends to be a process used by the company for the completion of those projects.

Some companies use a phase system, where the phases are descriptive as to tasks involved in the sequence of events leading to finished product.

For example a construction company may have a phase 1 that involves feasibility and costs, a phase 2 that looks at scheduling and value engineering, a phase 3 that focuses on materials and constructability, a phase 4 which is the bid process, and a phase 5 which is actual construction and product supervision to completion.

Within these phases are numerous tasks of varying importance, and project managers are making decisions every day, as to which tasks are most important, and often for multiple projects.

## THE SOLUTION

The only way effective way to teach these principles of prioritization is through mocking. We employ mocks of various kinds regularly, but in this context they provide incredible insight into what your team is thinking both in terms of the importance of tasks, but also who should be doing what, and when.

For maximum effectiveness, the person teaching the concepts should have five or six employees at a time. The employees should be directed to generate a list of the tasks they perform in a typical day without any context as to how that list will be used. That is all of the preparation needed for the training.

The instructor then meets with the group to walk through the decision matrix, define the relevant terms, and tie them to specific actions. This should be done in a generic fashion without using examples relevant to the group's professional work so as to prevent skewing their thoughts in any particular direction.

Once the concepts are covered, the instructor asks the group to take the lists they brought to the training, and categorize them into the four quadrants of the matrix.

After that is completed, the instructor calls for volunteers to walk through the tasks, and their thought processes for how each was determined. Asking the group for its thoughts on agreement, disagreement is a great way to get participation and determine the thoughts of everyone.

This process is a fantastic diagnostic for self-loaders, who rarely delegate even when they should (a common time management problem for top performing employees). Instructors often surprised as to the importance their team places on particular tasks, and this creates a fantastic dialogue to make sure all are on the same page

When the instructor has covered a couple of team members, we recommend rolling out the version of the matrix at attachment A, which is more detailed, and provides better clarity on timing and prioritization.

The instructor then calibrates the team as to what leadership's vision is on the varying importance of the tasks, and how they should properly be prioritized.

Finally, this method is most effective when team members actual begin to use the language of urgent/important, or urgent/non-important to describe expectations of teammates.

## TAKEAWAYS

- The Eisenhower Matrix is a Great Prioritization Tool

- Teaching it requires interactive exchange with team members applying their tasks in a setting with the leadership instructor.

# Chapter 3 The How - Part 2

"How did it get so late so soon?" – Dr. Seuss

We give in advance on this chapter as it may be unpopular with some of your folks. Efficient companies, responsible for the complex provision of products or services track time.

Often time tracking is used either for revenue documentation, or for determining costs. An architect, for example would need to justify its invoices (which are often a reflection of dollars per hour), and a pharmaceutical company may want to track how much labor went into the development of a particular drug in their portfolio.

THE PROBLEM:

Time tracking is often used for determining costs and revenue, but rarely as a diagnostic to evaluate effective time management by employees. In fact in some cases, time tracking rewards inefficiency!

THE EXAMPLE: ENGINEERING

Many engineering firms use time tracking for projects that are billed on a time and materials basis. Engineers who bill more time, are often considered top performers, and rewarded with bonuses and other accolades.

Rarely is there much analysis as to how top billers are spending their time. Some would argue that a business' purpose is to generate revenue to grow the business, and therefore high performing billers are essential. Both of those things are true, but if the high bills are a function of inefficiency (i.e. an employee taking 20 hours for what should have taken 5), your company is playing the short game. Long term, you will have upset clients, bad habits, and a team that takes longer because no one is stressing efficiency.

For our example, we can look to an engineering firm that focuses on acoustic designs for concert halls. Let's assume the company has a fixed fee contract, but and is not paid on an hourly basis. So long as they finish the job at or less than they priced it, they win right?

Not exactly. Even though the project came in at less than was bid, and the firm realized at or slightly more than the profit expected, there is no guarantee that the company's return on investment with staffing was maximized. In fact, we would argue that if there is no time tracking, there is a very could chance that roi (return on investment), was not maximized.

## THE SOLUTION

The solution is using time tracking, even informal time tracking for more than revenue calculation.

What is informal time tracking? Many companies that do not depend on the submission of time records for revenue use informal time tracking for a number of purposes.

For example, in engineering there is very often a bid process, and even when there isn't, engineering firms are issuing a price for their designs before work has begun. They typically do this using software, and often assumptions based on prior projects.

Informal time tracking allows for greater precision in that employees track their time in the office to projects. It can be done with a template that is submitted to leadership, or even a handwritten time sheet completed throughout the day, and submitted on Friday at the end of the week.

Other companies, including some top manufacturing firms have a card system, where computer access requires the use of an id card, and upon recognizing the user, requests that they choose a project. The software then tracks time for that employee from project to project. This is still informal, as the employee is not submitting specific descriptions of tasks or details. A variety of software is available to assist with this project documentation.

Formal time tracking would involve the use of time tracking software that tracks time, and tasks to specific phases of a project.

When employees are asked to track their time, there is often resistance in the ranks. From a messaging standpoint leadership should be clear, that they are using this information to make intelligent decisions about staffing, measure performance objectively to allow for deserved recognition and reward to top performers, and to allow for more precise information for use in competitively bidding jobs.

We recommend that team leads look at every team members' time going back a month, at least once a month. This is wealth of knowledge as to what folks are doing, how long it is taking, and what they are prioritizing. It allows for calibration, which when coupled with the material from chapter 2 can be very effective.

TAKEAWAYS

- Time tracking contains vastly more useful information than just revenue and cost information

- Time tracking can be formal or informal and both are useful if there is follow through

- Employee messaging should evolve around staffing, objective performance review and improving pricing for bidding

# Chapter 4 Slaying the Technology Dragon

"The first rule of any technology used in a business is that automation applied to an efficient operation will magnify the efficiency. The second is that automation applied to an inefficient operation will magnify the inefficiency."

— Bill Gates

Technology has wildly improved our efficiency, and then taken it all away with dazzling distractions.

THE PROBLEM

A recent study from salary.com, reported that 89% of employees reported wasting time at work **every day**!

Cheryl Conner in her piece *Wasting Time at Work: The Epidemic Continues,* reported that 31% waste roughly 30 minutes, another 31% wasted an hour, and another 26% waste 2-5 hours **per day**.

This does not include time wasted with inefficient review of emails and other technological distractions.

The constant disruption, and immediate need for the gratification of responding to all emails is a massive time waster. This is particularly true in the context of writing, or the use of management of highly precise data as in the accounting example below.

Employees must be taught to manage this distraction in an effective manner.

To further complicate matters, the newest generation of employees comes from a world that is often more comfortable with written communication, such as texting, which can be much less efficient than making a call.

## THE EXAMPLE

For purposes of this example we have chosen to address these issues in the context of an accounting firm. There are a number of businesses that don't require constant computer use, for which some of these examples may not apply, but accountants must be in front of the computer screen for most of the day, with the exception of time spent speaking to clients.

This job requires intense concentration and the accurate calculation and relocation of numbers in various spreadsheets constantly. The interruption of a phone beeped social network signal, or constant email popups, is enough to send the concentration of the most steadfast employee off the rails.

## THE SOLUTION

The first part of this problem is outright misuse of company time. As compared to the other time wasters we have covered so far, this is the first one which is intentional.

Every company should have a comprehensive internet appropriateness, and usage policy. We have provided the very useful and detailed free for use, SANS Internet Usage Policy as attachment B to this book. Editable electronic copies will be made available to readers at **ask@whatthegurusays.com**. This attachment also includes great procedures designed to warn the employee against other dangerous internet activities, that can create exposure and liability for the company.

We recommend having employees sign this document as part of their personnel file

Enforcement should also include an IT approved internet usage software, from which there are many to choose.

The problem of email, and phone popups such as texts, and app notifications is more complex. The employee is having to evaluate which to respond to, and when. This is further complicated by the fact that at the time the message came in, the employee was concentrated on a particular task, which he will have to revisit a few steps back to continue.

This distraction is a particularly difficult one for top performers who feel the need to instantly respond to a client or contact.

Leadership should discuss its expectations for the timeliness of responses. Checking email every two or three hours will, in the vast majority of cases, keep clients and contacts happy as to responsiveness, while allowing for the efficient completion of work.

Similarly, in dealing with younger professionals who are less comfortable with phone calls and in person meetings, stress the importance of relationships to your business, and explain how emails, no matter how well intentioned are impersonal, and reduce connectivity with clients.

Most systems also have means for allowing a beep or popup for certain VIP emails, or those that have been designated as urgent.

Internet usage policies must also take into account the expectations with regard to employee work hours. Those firms where employees typically work 10-12 hours or more, will have to be more lenient on the occasional personal email or setting of a doctor's appointment on company time.

Watch for employees who respond to quickly, or who send long emails that should have much more appropriately been handled as calls or in person discussions. The time wasted be these is wasted on both ends, because you in leadership are now having to unnecessarily long emails. If your employees need further review on this subject, we highly recommend *Speak Like a CEO* by Suzanne Bates.

TAKEAWAYS

- Have and Enforce a Practical Internet Usage Policy

- Give employees company expectations on response times that allow for reasonable completion of work

- Encourage employees to make calls instead of sending massive emails

# Chapter 5 Embracing What is Left of the Dragon

*"Should you find yourself in a chronically leaking boat, energy devoted to changing vessels is likely to be more productive than energy devoted to patching leaks."* – Warren Buffett

With technology, as with all things we must be careful not to throw out the good with the bad. There are great technologies for the improvement of time management that are simple, widely available, and not well used.

## THE PROBLEM

One of the greatest misconceptions about time management is that the "to-do" list improves effectiveness. Find any employee with constant time management issues, and his or her desk will be littered with post it notes on the monitor, lists with lines through items, and a stack of unfinished work. As Mr. Buffett suggests, it's time to change vessels.

## THE EXAMPLE

We have chosen law, and the work of lawyers and paralegals for this example, because these professionals serve many masters, have incredibly important deadlines, and responsibility for the completion of complex thoughtful tasks.

Lawyers and paralegals have to deal with clients in communicating the status and next steps in case preparation. They deal with Court's who make often immutable demands on the delivery of briefs and filing information. And they deal with opposing counsel, who regularly demands information, procedural responses, and other deliverables with which the lawyer must comply.

In this search for better time management, we found tons of lawyers using "to-do" lists, many of which had constant problems getting things done on time.

## THE SOLUTION

This seems obvious after the fact, but the solution is quite simple. Proper electronic calendaring. Many lawyers and other professionals use their calendars to remember key deadlines, important dates, etc. Few use calendars to their full potential.

A properly used calendar means never having another to do list ever again. Calendar entries allow for multidimensional use of task information.

A common problem with effective time management is misperceptions by the professional involved, as to how much time a task is going to take. Most "to do" lists don't even allocate for time, and there is not the instant feedback of realizing two or three times in a row that it is taking three hours to write a petition, and not two.

Instead of just teaching your people to calendar deadlines, have them allocate actual estimated time for the tasks they are performing. These may often have to be changed or revisited, but this provides employees with constant feedback as to how long it is taking to complete tasks.

If a calendar is used properly, there are several reviews which provide hugely important information.

In addition, your team leaders should have access to their team members' calendars, which allows for real time calibration.

If an employee is consistently taking too long to complete a task, it may indicate a need for further training or development. If an employee is scheduling calls, but not call prep time just before them, that may be a sign that the employee is not properly prepared. Calendars provide a wealth of information useful in diagnosing problems within a team

We recommend you teach your employees the following reviews:

1. Monthly review every Monday morning. Look to see what is coming in the next 30 days, to prevent surprises. If there are key deadlines you want to know well ahead of that, use your calendar. For example when a trial is scheduled, add a calendar entry for that date, 90 days out, 60 days out, and 30 days out, so that the reminders put the attorney on notice as time nears.

2. Weekly review every week day morning. Have your team look forward seven days to see what is coming and make the necessary arrangements to re-prioritize or delegate work so that it all gets done.

3. Daily review every day just before leaving. Have your team look back at the calendar for what didn't get done, and before leaving for the day, plug that task into the next few days based upon importance. This insures no task is dropped or forgotten about.

Of all of the diagnostic tools in this book, the calendar is one of the most important in assessing where your team is not just with respect to time management, but also with respect to competency and effectiveness.

## TAKEAWAYS

- The electronic calendar is a fantastic way to insure that your folks have all tasks properly planned both as to what must be done, but also how long it should take.

- Leaders should use their subordinate's calendars as a means of evaluating the prudence of how team time is being spent.

# Chapter 6 The Gardener Who Changed the World

*"Give me the fruitful error any time, full of seeds, bursting with its own corrections. You can keep your sterile truth for yourself."*
– Vilfredo Pareto

Vilfredo Pareto, the father of what we now know as the 80/20 rule noticed in the late 1890's that 80% of the peas in his garden were produced by 20% of the pea pods. A simple garden discovery, coupled with the mind of a world famous economist, has given rise to multiple applications of this principle to business, and leadership.

## THE PROBLEM

Employees, don't know which trees bare the low hanging fruit. Put another way, little thought is given to which relationships truly drive the business, so they spend massive amounts of virtually unproductive time with the wrong people. This is true in internally and externally.

## THE EXAMPLE: DISTRIBUTION

Internally, distribution is a complex, people and relationship driven business. Like other businesses, those in distribution must grow and attract phenomenal, talented employees, who are detail oriented, and care about clients, and making sure that all of the trains leave the station on time. What if your "people person," has problems with details? What if your best bean counter is afraid to talk to people?

Externally, whether the company is an auto parts supplier in the Northeast or a restaurant produce sourcer in the Midwest, there are multiple clients to please, all at the same time. Inventory management challenges, spikes and dips in demand, and the unpredictability of the needs of new clients complicate things further. Then, the distributor must always be looking for, or learning about new or better products to provide customers, to create that "stickiness," that keeps the customer around.

THE SOLUTION

Ignore what your mother told you. You know, that part about treating everyone equally? Obviously people should be given respect and common courtesy. That is not what this chapter is about.

Your time is an INVESTMENT. Both leadership and employees must see it that way. If anything, it is vastly more valuable than money. One would never look at the stock market, and say "I will split my money evenly over all stocks, performing and non-performing, because I don't want one of the stocks to feel bad." And yet that is exactly what we do with our time.

There is a common workplace paradox at time and tenure companies. These are companies, where seniority drives power, promotion, and influence within the company. Law firms are often guilty of this with their 8 year partnership tracks. Big companies often have cultures where promotion becomes a waiting game for your supervisor to be promoted or retire, so you can take that chair. This is ludicrous.

The paradox works like this, you have a top performer and a low-medium performer sitting next to each other in cubicles at your firm, each with equal tenure. People quickly notice the quality of work the top performer is doing, and send their most important projects to her. The people also learn that the low-medium performer does at best passable work, often with need of further revision. Suddenly the top performer is drowning, and the low-medium performer is cruising. Both are making the same money until their promotion to senior assistant, which takes two years.

The thing about top performers is that they almost universally have intelligence, urgency, and hunger. They will quickly tire of a world where their work doubles, and the pay is the same as the slacker next to them. Eventually, the performer will leave, and you will have an office full of slackers.

In teaching internal investment, employees must be taught that all will get the investment required for proper training to the point of competence. This is a function of fundamental fairness. If leadership focuses its attention on the individuals that are objectively performing at a higher level, as opposed apparent popularity, others will be incentivized to perform at that level.

Finally, abandon time and tenure. While loyalty over time is certainly valuable, a company doesn't grow if it doesn't promote and engage its top talent. This also creates a culture of investment, where leaders are actively looking to see which employees are making the biggest difference, and planning their investment around that.

Externally, the solution is similar. As crazy as it sounds all customers are not better for your business. An example from a few years ago was a produce distribution company on the gulf coast.

A particular restaurant's approach to selecting produce was to take a single grapefruit, or orange from the delivery, and cut it in half. If it did not meet the manager's specifications, he would reject the entire shipment. The grocer was agitated and complained about the situation, because he was hand selecting produce for this particular restaurant taking a great amount of time to separately package, and set aside product for this customer.

After a fairly short discussion, it became clear that the cost in labor and effort to satisfy this particular customer vastly exceeded the actual revenue generated by that relationship. While it is easy to applaud a restaurant manager for having such high standards, this grocer was using incredibly poor time management.

This is where the Pareto Principle comes into play. In many businesses, 80% or more of the revenue comes from roughly 20% of clients. That means many businesses spend four times the effort in their typical day chasing non-business driving revenue, than they do focusing on the customer profile that will drive growth. This information is vastly important to a sales team with finite time each weak to devote to bringing in new business.

Tim Ferriss in his book *The 4 Hour Work*, uses a great example from one of his own businesses. Tim had a supplement company that was taking off, and he was working incredible hours to keep all of his customer's happy. Introspectively, he looked at what customers were actually driving his brand, and how much time was being spent taking care of them, and cultivating other companies like them. He was somewhat surprised to learn that many of his most difficult time consuming client relationships were not moving the needle on his business. So he dropped them.

That seems like a dramatic thing to do, and it didn't happen quite so quickly as that. He formulated a view of what criteria he wanted from his clients, and then pushed his clients toward that criteria to continue the relationship. Many, who were not doing much business, picked up their purchasing to qualify, which also helped his business!

The point is that this view of time as a fungible investment, changes how people make decisions, and it will dramatically increase productivity.

As a final note, much has been written on applying the Pareto Principle to other subjects, such as learning language, basic mastery of musical instruments etc. If the focus is on learning the key concepts, development speed goes through the roof in a time efficient way. This is a fantastic time management tool!

## TAKEAWAYS

- The 80/20 has incredible applicability to your business and time management

- Think of your time as an incredibly important investment. Pick your stocks (people) wisely

- Not all clients are great for your business

# Chapter 7  Why Your Top Performers Don't Delegate And How to Fix it.

"A particular shot or way of moving the ball can be a player's personal signature, but efficiency of performance is what wins the game for the team." – Pat Riley

It is cliché for leaders to talk about how they would like to clone their top performers, or how they wish they had 20 of Joe or Suzy. The simple reality is that as brilliant as the typical top performer is, it is also very common for them to miss the mark on time management.

## THE PROBLEM

Top performers tend to have particular traits almost universally. They tend to have intense hunger to learn the craft, good to great focus, an alpha mentality, work ethic, and a constant sense of urgency. Unfortunately they also tend to have issues with self-loading, and the perception that none can do things as well as they can, which leads to poor delegation of non-critical tasks, and huge inefficiency.

## THE EXAMPLE: CONSULTING

Consultants must work in teams, and high performers, whether they be on the key client contact side, or in business development, typically find themselves juggling large numbers of small tasks. Often these tasks could much more effectively be handled by others, including those training under your performers, and or administrative assistants.

These tasks often include gathering and processing massive amounts of information for purposes of running the calculations necessary to provide the recommendations the client has requested. The recommendations often come in the form of a report which may require extensive writing.

Your best consultants will have the ability to pivot, thinking quickly on their toes, as well as the ability to command the situation. They instill confidence, letting your clients know there is a plan, and that it will bring value in excess of the cost of consulting. Finally, these folks are your best firemen. They can handle the difficult calls, while maintaining and often improving the client relationship.

It is a fail for those with these skills to be spending time in mundane calculations, or editing reports. The problem is that the DNA in these performers gives them the belief that they must do everything to properly serve the client. This is the belief you must break.

THE SOLUTION

The solution in this situation is process. Your performers must be given a clear workflow, specific to the creation of the promised deliverable. Your process should include not only tasks, but personnel assignments, and timeline expectations, which can be shared with the client to assist in managing expectations.

This accomplishes a couple of things. First, it allows for your talented top performers to maximize their time, freeing them up for key calls to develop and improve client service. Second, depending on skillset, it frees up your performers to develop others (who gain familiarity with the process by taking on the simple tasks first, and evolving based upon the trainee's talents to more complex work).

Following the approach gives your new employees a logical process to follow, providing clarity on the steps required to reach the point of your high performers, which should be the goal for all of your new folks.

Third, this creates consistency within your firm in terms of quality and the characteristics of the deliverable. We have provided a simple consulting workflow to illustrate these concepts at Attachment C. If you are interested in reading more on the massive impact good process can bring, check out *Switch: How to Change Things, When Change is Hard*, by Chip and Dan Heath.

A word of caution. Clear well developed processes will have an incredible impact on speed, and free up your most talented people to their best use. However, if they are not governed properly, processes can stifle creativity. This must be monitored, and employees must be constantly encouraged to use their creative ideas to improve the process, and the product. Otherwise, your deliverable can become a template. This weakens the value you bring to a client, who could just as easily follow the template if every deliverable is the same.

## TAKEAWAYS

- Getting the most out of your performers means breaking bad habits on self-loading and teaching them how to delegate

- Great processes provide team-wide clarity as to task, personnel, and timing

- If used correctly, this approach creates a great breeding ground for training and developing new talent

# Chapter 8 The Waiter's Secret to Telephone Time Management

*"If you don't know where you are going, you'll end up someplace else."*
– Yogi Berra

Have you ever been in a restaurant with a struggling waiter? Maybe you have noticed other waiters calmly handling tables while your waiter seems frenetic, running from place to place. The reason for that is the secret known by all good waiters (to be discussed below).

## THE PROBLEM

Your employees spend too much time bouncing from call to call, or endlessly responding to email strings, only to find no time left in the day, with not much done.

## THE EXAMPLE: INSURANCE

Insurance professionals are in constant communication mode. Whether the issue is reviewing new coverages to match a client's particular needs, or calling various carriers to procure coverage that meets those needs, an insurance agent is constantly on the phone or at the computer.

This is also true when it comes to submitting claims which require substantial detail to process. Agency owners constantly bemoan how one professional can get so much done, and the person next to her seems to struggle, given exactly the same amount of time and tools.

## THE SOLUTION

The great waiter watches the poor waiter run to a table, and back to the kitchen, then back with water from the kitchen, and then off to the next table to repeat the process. The great waiter goes to each table in circulation, determining what is needed, makes one trip to the kitchen, and returns with the needs of multiple tables. Ironically, this waiter is working less, and probably with less frustration in his guests, making more money.

The secret is consolidation. It seems simple enough, but in practice it is rare.

Applied to our insurance professionals, this means more thoughtful interaction. An uber productive agent advised that he "treated client calls as though this was the last time he would get to speak to them." That kind of philosophy means fewer calls, and more productive calls.

It requires simple planning, with that "what if this is my last chance to communicate," mentality. As employees get more experienced, the planning they tend to do actually decreases. If managers are spot checking calendars as described above, they can quickly see a trend of calendared calls with no prep time. This minor prior planning makes a huge difference in efficiency.

If phone calls are a time waster, emails are a time killer. A McKinsey Global Institute study called *The social economy: Unlocking value and productivity through social technologies*, found that employees spent on average 28% of their time reviewing and responding to emails. The study recommended more effective use of collaboration tools, such as team project software, to reduce emails.

We have already provided tips on more efficient use of email time, but consolidation makes a difference here as well. The same planning that considers all of the possible needs that could be met at the time the email was sent, will reduce the number interruptions both for employees, and for your clients.

## TAKEAWAYS

- Basic call and email planning means fewer calls and better use of client and employee time.

- 28% of employee time is spent reading and responding to email

# Chapter 9 Sharpening the Ax

"If I had nine hours to chop down a tree, I would spend the first six sharpening the ax." – Abraham Lincoln

One of the most common traits among legendarily efficient people is a morning routine.

## THE PROBLEM

Your team starts the work day with insufficient physical and mental preparation.

## THE EXAMPLE: BUSINESS LEADERS

Leaders of the largest companies manage an incredible amount of information, numerous decisions, and the drive to handle it all is often internal. These routines are critical to the effectiveness for which these luminaries are known.

There are a number of commonalities in the way the world's best leaders prepare to take on the world.

Wildly successful titans of business consistently exercise in the morning. A few examples of well-respected business leaders using this as part of their morning routine include for example: Howard Schultz (CEO of Starbucks), Ursula Burns (CEO of Xerox), Jack Dorsey (Founder of Square, and co-founder of twitter), and Tim Cook (Apple CEO).

Another common part of the routine for many of these leaders is rising early. In addition to the leaders referenced above, the following leaders get an advantage on most by giving themselves extra time in the day: Tim Armstrong (AOL CEO), Padmassre Warrior (Cisco's former Chief Technology Officer),

Another important use of this morning time common to executive leadership is some form of reflection. Often, this takes the form of meditation, though many leaders claim that the time taken for hikes, or jogging helps improve clarity of thought. Examples of those that use this technique include: Paul English (co-founder of Kayak and Blade), Ray Dalio (CEO of Bridgewater the world's largest hedge fund), and Oprah Winfrey (Billionaire TV personality).

Common to a number of time management rituals is a consistent pattern of sleep. Elon Musk (Founder of Tesla), Richard Branson (Founder of Virgin), and Marissa Mayer, (CEO of Yahoo), tend to be at the low end with six hours of sleep per night. Our research revealed that the most common number of hours of sleep on a regular basis was seven. Bill Gates, Tim Cook, and Jeff Bezos report regularly receiving 7 hours of sleep. A number of recent studies suggest that at least 7 hours of sleep on a consistent basis are required for optimal performance.

Finally, many of the world's most successful people, start their days the night before, with a plan. The idea is that one of the final things great time managers do before their day ends is to plan and set goals for the next day. Examples include: Kenneth Chenault (CEO of American Express), Benjamin Franklin (founding father of the United States), Scott Stouffer (founder of Market Brew and Salsa Labs).

THE SOLUTION

So how do you get your people to emulate these important behaviors?

First, there must be very basic education what the successful habits are. There are a number of great examples in the section above, but ultimately it is not enough to simply tell your folks about these habits.

Modern firms must have a wellness mindset. That can be as simple as sponsoring regular wellness related events, such as 5k's, and local bike riding events, exercise groups etc. Many medium sized firms have small gyms, and or wellness officers charged with making healthy snack, and workout options available to employees.

These changes are often less expensive than you would imagine, and some allow for reductions in the cost of health insurance for your firm. Some insurance carriers offer their customers access to wellness information designed to help them make better, better educated decisions.

There have been a number of studies on the impact of wellness on organizations, and their outcomes are consistent. Wellness positively impacts employee engagement with the company, overall health, retention, and productivity.

Leonard Barry of Harvard Business Review, wrote an article entitled *What's the Hard Return on Employee Wellness Programs?* Citing numerous corporate examples. Johnson and Johnson estimated that their wellness program saved the company $250 million dollars, returning every dollar of investment with a return of $2.71.

MD Anderson Cancer Center in Houston implemented a wellness program that reduced missed time by employees by 80%.

Nelnet, one of the nation's largest student loan servicing companies reported that in exit interviews, when asked what the employee would miss most about the company, the number one answer was its wellness program.

In addition to wellness, your middle managers should spend time counseling their employees on planning techniques. Teams should have a meeting early in the week to discuss what the goals of the group are, and the calendaring and planning techniques discussed herein, should be taught and reviewed.

Productivity, engagement, and the overall health care costs of your organization will improve. For further consideration, read *The Miracle Morning*, by Hal Elrod

TAKEAWAYS:

- Teach employees wellness habits such as proper exercise, and reflection routines in the morning

- Proper sleep, often a problem for young people, is critical to continuous solid production

- Planning the night before, or early morning as to what is to be accomplished is critical to focus

## Chapter 10 The Quiet Danger of Superfluous Choices

"Everything must be made as simple as possible. But not simpler." — Albert Einstein

The best leaders in the world surround themselves with incredibly smart people, and use a methodical approach to decision making.

One of the biggest time management mistakes we see is poor approach to decision making. This is not a function of how long it takes to make decisions. It is more a function of when we make decisions, and our state at the time we do.

## PROBLEM

Decision fatigue is real, and if you are not mindful as to teaching your people how to avoid it, your business will suffer.

## THE EXAMPLE: MEDICINE

As the day proceeds our mental acuity and ability to make decisions is depleted. This is a well-documented phenomenon in numerous human contexts.

Decision fatigue was first identified by **Dr. Roy F. Baumeister,** who demonstrated that humans have a finite store of mental energy for making decisions, which can be broken down into what he called the **Rubicon model of action phases.** He determined that all decision making fell into four basic categories, which he described as:

1. Predecisional Phase – assessing wishes and forming intended goal

2. **Preactional Phase / Making a Decision** – planning and choosing goal-directed actions

3. Actional Phase – implementing chosen actions

4. Postactional Phase – evaluating whether goal was achieved

Following Dr. Baumeister's analysis a bit further, decision making even in simple contexts, is a higher brain function, which causes a phenomenon called "ego depletion," which builds, and leads to fatigue that ultimately impacts choices, and the quality of decisions.

The problem of decision fatigue syndrome is rarely more dangerous than in the world of medicine. The reality is that the current challenges of advanced technology, and competing theories on medicine and treatment options, coupled with the often time-limited requirements on decision making from doctors, create a dangerous environment for patient care.

In their study on decision fatigue specific to medicine called *Time of Day and the Decision to Prescribe Antibiotics,* Dr. Jeffrey A. Linder, found that doctors are more likely to prescribe unnecessary antibiotics as the day progresses.

In their book, *Decision Making in Health and Medicine: Integrating Evidence and Values* By M. G. Myriam Hunink, Milton C. Weinstein, Eve Wittenberg, Michael F. Drummond, Joseph S. Pliskin, John B. Wong, Paul P. Glasziou, call for a systematic approach to decision making that reduces the chance for such mistakes.

While very dangerous in the medical context, this phenomenon is by no means limited to doctors. An oft cited study published study by the National Academy of Sciences, found that later in the day, judges were less likely to sentence convicted criminals to parole. In fact, regardless of the crime at issue, judges were 65% more likely to rule favorably. This number decreased as the day progressed to lunch, where upon the return from lunch, the number was 65% again. Then as the day ebbed, this number decreased demonstrably.

If you wish to make the most of time management, you must teach your people when and under what circumstances to make important decisions.

All of this is very good for realizing that we make worse decisions as the day progresses. So what do you do?

SOLUTION

As in the other examples, awareness is the first step to teaching your folks. We have attached a graphic illustrating the above referenced Rubicon for that purpose.

There are also a number of important techniques for reducing decision fatigue, and insuring your folks make the most of their time.

The first technique is to work to make important decisions early in the day. This should become a part of the planning described earlier in this book. This simple technique also reduces procrastination. In his best seller *Eat That Frog*, Brian Tracy espouses the importance of taking on the most difficult items and decisions early in the day.

The second approach is to limit the options. More than three options for solving a problem causes analysis paralysis, and requires decisions stacked on other decisions. Require that those coming to you for decisions, bring proposed options and solutions. This is good training for your people, and reduces your fatigue.

Third, if the decision doesn't need to be made by you personally, or doesn't need to be made today, no matter the temptation, don't make it. Teach your people to conserve their finite decision making resources for the tasks which require them. A number of business leaders have taken this to the extreme. Consider Steve Jobs, whose wardrobe was almost completely identical. Other leaders eat the same lunch virtually every day, so as to avoid the need for superfluous decisions.

Fourth, teach your team to make their first decision work. Constant revisiting of options, even after they have been made is not productive, and can cause massive inefficiency.

Finally, apply principles of triage. During the civil war, doctors were constantly faced with the need to rapidly stabilize patients as quickly as possible. The idea became known as meatball surgery, and the concept of "save them now, make them pretty later," has a ton of applicability in the business world.

Perfectionism is the enemy of time management, and it is exceptionally rarely required. Quality is important to every organization, but a common problem in high performers is the need to perform beyond reasonable quality standards required for the application. This has a negative impact on effectiveness.

## Conclusion

As you have seen, the concepts in this book are intertwined. They are powerful, and simple tools that can be employed to improve how your people use their most valuable commodity.

We have gathered these techniques from the thought leaders on the issue, and most well respected leaders in the country. These folks get maximum return for their time investment, by making these techniques habit. Good luck on your journey to getting the most out of your people!

## Congratulations!

I'm very grateful that you took the time to read this book. So I wanted to add more value! If you send your email to **ask@whatthegurusays.com**, I will send you some information on apps, many of them free, to help with time management.

I am not big on harassing you with offers, and promise not to bomb your email, but as we update and improve our leadership offerings, I want to share that with those who have taken the time to read our work.

Regards,

- John   Founder of The Guru Series

Attachment A

The Eisenhower Decision Matrix

|  | Urgent | Not Urgent |
|---|---|---|
| **Important** | 1. Highest Priority<br><br>**Do**<br><br>Things that must be done **now** | 2. Medium Priority<br><br>**Decide**<br><br>Things that you must do, but **not now** |
| **Not Important** | 3. Medium Priority<br><br>**Delegate**<br><br>Things that are not the best use of your time but **must be done** | 4. Low Priority<br><br>**Delete**<br><br>Things that you shouldn't be doing at all |

Attachment B

# Internet Usage Policy

1. Overview

Internet connectivity presents the company with new risks that must be addressed to safeguard the facility's vital information assets. These risks include: Access to the Internet by personnel that is inconsistent with business needs results in the misuse of resources. These activities may adversely affect productivity due to time spent using or "surfing" the Internet. Additionally, the company may face loss of reputation and possible legal action through other types of misuse. All information found on the Internet should be considered suspect until confirmed by another reliable source. There is no quality control process on the Internet, and a considerable amount of its information is outdated or inaccurate. Access to the Internet will be provided to users to support business activities and only on an as needed basis to perform their jobs and professional roles.

2. Purpose

The purpose of this policy is to define the appropriate uses of the Internet by employees and affiliates.

3. Scope

The Internet usage Policy applies to all Internet users (individuals working for the company, including permanent full-time and part-time employees, contract workers, temporary agency workers, business partners, and vendors) who access the Internet through the computing or networking resources. The company's Internet users are expected to be familiar with and to comply with this policy, and are also required to use their common sense and exercise their good judgment while using Internet services.

3.1 Internet Services

Internet access is to be used for business purposes only. Capabilities for the following standard Internet services will be provided to users as needed:

> • E-mail -- Send/receive E-mail messages to/from the Internet (with or without document attachments).
> • Navigation -- WWW services as necessary for business purposes, using a hypertext transfer protocol (HTTP) browser tool. Full access to the Internet; limited access from the Internet to dedicated company public web servers only.
>
> • File Transfer Protocol (FTP) -- Send data/files and receive in-bound data/files, as necessary for business purposes.

- Telnet -- Standard Internet protocol for terminal emulation. User Strong Authentication required for Internet initiated contacts into the company. Management reserves the right to add or delete services as business needs change or conditions warrant. All other services will be considered unauthorized access to/from the Internet and will not be allowed.

## 3.2 Request & Approval Procedures

Internet access will be provided to users to support business activities and only as needed to perform their jobs.

## 3.3 Request for Internet Access

As part of the Internet access request process, the employee is required to read both this Internet usage Policy and the associated Internet/Intranet Security Policy the user must then sign the statements (located on the last page of each document) that he/she understands and agrees to comply with the policies. Users not complying with these policies could be subject to disciplinary action up to and including termination. Policy awareness and acknowledgment, by signing the acknowledgment form, is required before access will be granted.

## 3.3 Approval

Internet access is requested by the user or user's manager submitting an IT Access Request form to the IT department along with an attached copy of a signed Internet usage Coverage Acknowledgment Form.

## 3.4 Removal of privileges

Internet access will be discontinued upon termination of employee, completion of contract, end of service of non-employee, or disciplinary action arising from violation of this policy. In the case of a change in job function and/or transfer the original access code will be discontinued, and only reissued if necessary and a new request for access is approved.

All user IDs that have been inactive for thirty (30) days will be revoked. The privileges granted to users must be reevaluated by management annually. In response to feedback from management, systems administrators must promptly revoke all privileges no longer needed by users.

# 4 Policy

## 4.1 Resource Usage

Access to the Internet will be approved and provided only if reasonable business needs are identified. Internet services will be granted based on an employee's current job responsibilities. If an employee moves to another business unit or changes job functions, a new Internet access request must be submitted within 5 days.

## 4.2 Allowed Usage

Internet usage is granted for the sole purpose of supporting business activities necessary to carry out job functions. All users must follow the corporate principles regarding resource usage and exercise good judgment in using the Internet. Questions can be addressed to the IT Department. Acceptable use of the Internet for performing job functions might include:

- Communication between employees and non-employees for business purposes;

- IT technical support downloading software upgrades and patches;

- Review of possible vendor web sites for product information; • Reference regulatory or technical information.

- Research

4.3 Personal Usage

Using company computer resources to access the Internet for personal purposes, without approval from the user's manager and the IT department, may be considered cause for disciplinary action up to and including termination.

All users of the Internet should be aware that the company network creates an audit log reflecting request for service, both in-bound and out-bound addresses, and is periodically reviewed. Users who choose to store or transmit personal information such as private keys, credit card numbers or certificates or make use of Internet "wallets" do so at their own risk.

The company is not responsible for any loss of information, such as information stored in the wallet, or any consequential loss of personal property

4.4 Prohibited Usage

Information stored in the wallet, or any consequential loss of personal property. Acquisition, storage, and dissemination of data which is illegal, pornographic, or which negatively depicts race, sex or creed is specifically prohibited.

The company also prohibits the conduct of a business enterprise, political activity, engaging in any form of intelligence collection from our facilities, engaging in fraudulent activities, or knowingly disseminating false or otherwise libelous materials. Other activities that are strictly prohibited include, but are not limited to:

- Accessing company information that is not within the scope of one's work. This includes unauthorized reading of customer account information, unauthorized access of personnel file information, and accessing information that is not needed for the proper execution of job functions.

- Misusing, disclosing without proper authorization, or altering customer or personnel information. This includes making unauthorized changes to a personnel file or sharing electronic customer or personnel data with unauthorized personnel.

- Deliberate pointing or hyper-linking of company Web sites to other Internet/WWW sites whose content may be inconsistent with or in violation of the aims or policies of the company.

- Any conduct that would constitute or encourage a criminal offense, lead to civil liability, or otherwise violate any regulations, local, state, national or international law including without limitations US export control laws and regulations.

- Use, transmission, duplication, or voluntary receipt of material that infringes on the copyrights, trademarks, trade secrets, or patent rights of any person or organization. Assume that all materials on the Internet are copyright and/or patented unless specific notices state otherwise.

- Transmission of any proprietary, confidential, or otherwise sensitive information without the proper controls.

- Creation, posting, transmission, or voluntary receipt of any unlawful, offensive, libelous, threatening, harassing material, including but not limited to comments based on race, national origin, sex, sexual orientation, age, disability, religion, or political beliefs.
- Any form of gambling. Unless specifically authorized under the provisions of this agreement.

The following activities are also strictly prohibited:

- Unauthorized downloading of any shareware programs or files for use without authorization in advance from the IT Department and the user's manager.

- Any ordering (shopping) of items or services on the Internet.

- Playing of any games.

- Forwarding of chain letters.

- Participation in any on-line contest or promotion.

- Acceptance of promotional gifts.

Bandwidth both within the company and in connecting to the Internet is a shared, finite resource. Users must make reasonable efforts to use this resource in ways that do not negatively affect other employees.

Specific departments may set guidelines on bandwidth use and resource allocation, and may ban the downloading of particular file types.

## 4.5 Software License

The Company strongly supports strict adherence to software vendors' license agreements. When at work, or when company computing or networking resources are employed, copying of software in a manner not consistent with the vendor's license is strictly forbidden.

Questions regarding lawful versus unlawful copying should be referred to the IT Department for review or to request a ruling from the Legal Department before any copying is done. Similarly, reproduction of materials available over the Internet must be done only with the written permission of the author or owner of the document.

Unless permission from the copyright owner(s) is first obtained, making copies of material from magazines, journals, newsletters, other publications and online documents is forbidden unless this is both reasonable and customary. This notion of "fair use" is in keeping with international copyright laws.

Using company computer resources to access the Internet for personal purposes, without approval from the user's manager and the IT department, may be considered cause for disciplinary action up to and including termination.

All users of the Internet should be aware that the company network creates an audit log reflecting request for service, both in-bound and out-bound addresses, and is periodically reviewed.

Users who choose to store or transmit personal information such as private keys, credit card numbers or certificates or make use of Internet "wallets" do so at their own risk.

4.6 Review of Public Information

All publicly-writeable directories on Internet-connected computers will be reviewed and cleared each evening. This process is necessary to prevent the anonymous exchange of information inconsistent with company business. Examples of unauthorized public information include pirated information, passwords, credit card numbers, and pornography.

4.7 Expectation of Privacy

4.7.1 Monitoring

Users should consider their Internet activities as periodically monitored and limit their activities accordingly. Management reserves the right to examine E-mail, personal file directories, web access, and other information stored on company computers, at any time and without notice. This examination ensures compliance with internal policies and assists with the management of company information systems.

4.7.2 E-mail Confidentiality Users should be aware that clear text E-mail is not a confidential means of communication. The company cannot guarantee that electronic communications will be private.

Employees should be aware that electronic communications can, depending on the technology, be forwarded, intercepted, printed, and stored by others.

Users should also be aware that once an E-mail is transmitted it may be altered. Deleting an E-mail from an individual workstation will not eliminate it from the various systems across which it has been transmitted.

4.7 Maintaining Corporate Image

4.8.1 Representation

When using company resources to access and use the Internet, users must realize they represent the company. Whenever employees state an affiliation to the company, they must also clearly indicate that "the opinions expressed are my own and not necessarily those of the company". Questions may be addressed to the IT Department.

4.8.2 Company Materials

Users must not place company material (examples: internal memos, press releases, product or usage information, documentation, etc.) on any mailing list, public news group, or such service.

Any posting of materials must be approved by the employee's manager and the public relations department and will be placed by an authorized individual.

4.8.3 Creating Web Sites All individuals and/or business units wishing to establish a WWW home page or site must first develop business, implementation, and maintenance plans.

Formal authorization must be obtained through the IT Department. This will maintain publishing and content standards needed to ensure consistency and appropriateness. In addition, contents of the material made available to the public through the Internet must be formally reviewed and approved before being published. All material should be submitted to the Corporate Communications Directors for initial approval to continue. All company pages are owned by, and are the ultimate responsibility of, the Corporate Communications Directors. All company web sites must be protected from unwanted intrusion through formal security measures which can be obtained from the IT department.

4.9 Periodic Reviews

4.9.1 Usage Compliance Reviews To ensure compliance with this policy, periodic reviews will be conducted. These reviews will include testing the degree of compliance with usage policies.

4.9.2 Policy Maintenance Reviews Periodic reviews will be conducted to ensure the appropriateness and the effectiveness of usage policies. These reviews may result in the modification, addition, or deletion of usage policies to better suit company information needs.

## 5. Policy Compliance

### 5.1 Compliance Measurement

I.T. team will verify compliance to this policy through various methods, including but not limited to, business tool reports, internal and external audits, and feedback to company leadership.

### 5.2 Exceptions
Any exception to the policy must be approved by IT.

### 5.3 Non-Compliance
An employee found to have violated this policy may be subject to disciplinary action, up to and including termination of employment. Additionally, the company may at its discretion seek legal remedies for damages incurred as a result of any violation.

The company may also be required by law to report certain illegal activities to the proper enforcement agencies. Before access to the Internet via company network is approved, the potential Internet user is required to read this Internet usage Policy and sign an acknowledgment form (located on the last page of this document). The signed acknowledgment form should be turned in and will be kept on file at the facility granting the access. For questions on the Internet usage Policy, contact the Information Technology (IT) Department.

## 6. INTERNET APPROPRIATE USAGE COVERAGE ACKNOWLEDGMENT FORM

After reading this policy, please sign the coverage form and submit it to your facility's IT department or granting facility's IT department for filing.

By signing below, the individual requesting Internet access through company computing resources hereby acknowledges receipt of and compliance with the Internet Usage Policy.

Furthermore, the undersigned also acknowledges that he/she has read and understands this policy before signing this form. Internet access will not be granted until this acknowledgment form is signed by the individual's manager.

After completion, the form is filed in the individual's human resources file (for permanent employees), or in a folder specifically dedicated to Internet access (for contract workers, etc.), and maintained by the IT department.

These acknowledgment forms are subject to internal audit.

## ACKNOWLEDGMENT

I have read the Internet Usage Policy. I understand the contents, and I agree to comply with the said Policy.

Location (Location and address)

Signature _____

Date _____

Manager/Supervisor

Signature_____

Date _____

# Attachment C

## Consulting Work Flow

| | |
|---|---|
| Phase 1 | **DISCUSS ORGANIZATIONAL ISSUES**<br><br>These are high level discussions with key members of client's leadership team to assess the situation. (15-30 Days) |
| Phase 2 | **ANALYZE THE PROBLEM**<br><br>This is data analysis from document gathering and follow up interviews designed for more intimate familiarity with the issue. (60-90 Days) |
| Phase 3 | **STRATEGY/RECOMMENDATIONS**<br><br>Internal determination of options, with pros and cons analysis as to which is best and why. (15-30 Days) |
| Phase 4 | **IMPLEMENTATION**<br><br>Consultant shares the solution vision, works through management and leadership logistics with client, and breaks down implementation (30-60 Days) |
| Phase 5 | **RESULTS REVIEW/FOLLOW UP**<br><br>Series of monthly informal reviews to insure the process is rolled out to maximize results (30-120 Days) |

# Attachment D

## Rubicon Model of Action Phases

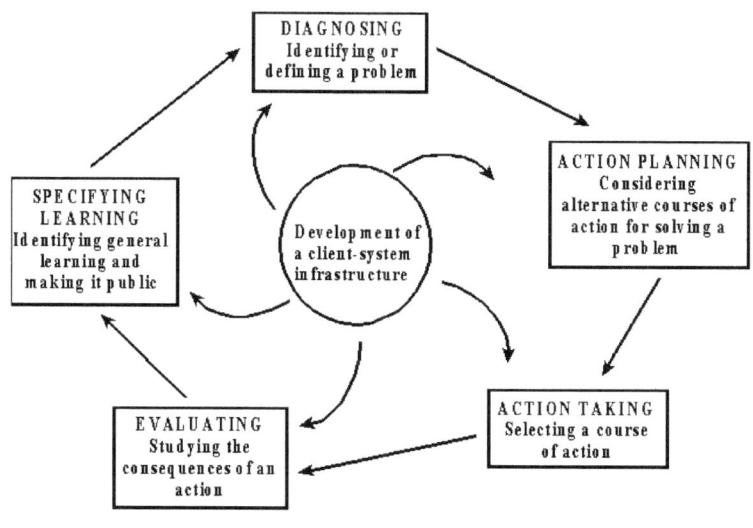

# Recommended Reading

*Raving Fans*, by Ken Blanchard

*Seven Habits of Highly Effective People*, by Steven Covey

*The 4 Hour Workweek*, by Timothy Ferriss

*Speak Like a CEO* by Suzanne Bates.

*Switch: How to Change Things, When Change is Hard*, by Chip and Dan Heath.

*The social economy: Unlocking value and productivity through social technologies*, by McKinsey Global Institute.

*The Miracle Morning*, by Hal Elrod

*Decision Making in Health and Medicine: Integrating Evidence and Values* by M. G. Myriam Hunink, Milton C. Weinstein, Eve Wittenberg, Michael F. Drummond, Joseph S. Pliskin, John B. Wong, Paul P. Glasziou

*Eat That Frog*, by Brian Tracy